Feeling

is the

Secret

by

Neville Goddard

&

The
Strangest Secret

by

Earl Nightingale

Copyright © 2024 Merchant Books

ISBN 978-1-60386-906-5

DIGITALIZED BY
WATCHMAKER PUBLISHING
ALL RIGHTS RESERVED

Table *of* Contents

Feeling is the Secret

Foreword	4
Chapter 1 Law & Its Operation	5
Chapter 2 Sleep	11
Chapter 3 Prayer	17
Chapter 4 Spirit – Feeling	21

The Strangest Secret

Text *of the* Audio Version	25
Text *of the* Video Version	45

Foreword

This book is concerned with the art of realizing your desire. It gives you an account of the mechanism used in the production of the visible world. It is a small book but not slight. There is a treasure in it, a clearly defined road to the realization of your dreams.

Were it possible to carry conviction to another by means of reasoned arguments and detailed instances, this book would be many times its size. It is seldom possible, however, to do so by means of written statements or arguments since to the suspended judgment it always seems plausible to say that the author was dishonest or deluded, and, therefore, his evidence was tainted. Consequently, I have purposely omitted all arguments and testimonials, and simply challenge the open-minded reader to practice the law of consciousness as revealed in this book.

Personal success will prove far more convincing than all the books that could be written on the subject.

NEVILLE

Chapter 1

Law & Its Operation

The world, and all within it, is man's conditioned consciousness objectified. Consciousness is the cause as well as the substance of the entire world. So it is to consciousness that we must turn if we would discover the secret of creation.

Knowledge of the law of consciousness and the method of operating this law will enable you to accomplish all you desire in life. Armed with a working knowledge of this law, you can build and maintain an ideal world.

Consciousness is the one and only reality, not figuratively but actually. This reality may for the sake of clarity be likened unto a stream which is divided into two parts, the conscious and the subconscious. In order to intelligently operate the law of consciousness, it is necessary to understand the relationship between the conscious and the subconscious. The conscious is personal and selective; the subconscious is impersonal and non-selective. The conscious is the realm of effect; the subconscious is the realm of cause. These two aspects are the male and female divisions of consciousness. The conscious is male; the subconscious is female.

The conscious generates ideas and impresses these ideas on the subconscious; the subconscious receives ideas and gives form and expression to them.

By this law – first conceiving an idea and then impressing the idea conceived on the subconscious – all things evolve out of consciousness; and without this sequence, there is not anything made that is made. The conscious impresses the subconscious, while the subconscious expresses all that is impressed upon it.

The subconscious does not originate ideas, but accepts as true those which the conscious mind feels to be true and, in a way known only to itself, objectifies the accepted ideas. Therefore, through his power to imagine and feel and his freedom to choose the idea he will entertain, man has control over creation. Control of the subconscious is accomplished through control of your ideas and feelings.

The mechanism of creation is hidden in the very depth of the subconscious, the female aspect or womb of creation. The subconscious transcends reason and is independent of induction. It contemplates a feeling as a fact existing within itself and on this assumption proceeds to give expression to it. The creative process begins with an idea and its cycle runs its course as a feeling and ends in a volition to act.

Ideas are impressed on the subconscious through the medium of feeling. No idea can be impressed on the subconscious until it is felt, but once felt – be it good, bad or indifferent – it must be expressed. Feeling is the one and only medium through which ideas are conveyed to the subconscious. Therefore, the man who does not control his feeling may easily impress the subconscious with undesirable states. By control of feeling is not meant restraint or suppression of your feeling, but rather the disciplining of self to imagine and entertain only such feeling as contributes to your happiness. Control of your feeling is all important to a full and happy life. Never entertain an undesirable feeling, nor think sympathetically about wrong in any shape or form. Do not dwell on the imperfection of yourself or others. To do so is to impress the subconscious with these limitations. What you do not want done unto you, do not feel that it is done unto you or another. This is the whole law of a full and happy life. Everything else is commentary.

Every feeling makes a subconscious impression and, unless it is counteracted by a more powerful feeling of an opposite nature, must be expressed. The dominant of two feelings is the one expressed. *I am healthy* is a stronger feeling than *I will be healthy*. To feel *I will be* is to confess *I am not*; *I am* is stronger than *I am not*.

What you feel *you are* always dominates what you feel *you would like to be*; therefore, to be realized, the wish must be felt as *a state that is* rather than *a state that is not*.

Sensation precedes manifestation and is the foundation upon which all manifestation rests. Be careful of your moods and feelings, for there is an unbroken connection between your feelings and your visible world. Your body is an emotional filter and bears the unmistakable marks of your prevalent emotions. Emotional disturbances, especially suppressed emotions, are the causes of all disease. To feel intensely about a wrong without voicing or expressing that feeling is the beginning of disease – disease – in both body and environment. Do not entertain the feeling of regret or failure for frustration or detachment from your objective results in disease.

Think feelingly only of the state you desire to realize. Feeling the reality of the state sought and living and acting on that conviction is the way of all seeming miracles. All changes of expression are brought about through a change of feeling. A change of feeling is a change of destiny. All creation occurs in the domain of the subconscious. What you must acquire, then, is a reflective control of the operation of the subconscious, that is, control of your ideas and feelings.

Chance or accident is not responsible for the things that happen to you, nor is predestined fate the author of your fortune or misfortune. Your subconscious impressions determine the conditions of your world. The subconscious is not selective; it is impersonal and no respecter of persons *(Romans 2:11)*. The subconscious is not concerned with the truth or falsity of your feeling. It always accepts as true that which you feel to be true. Feeling is the assent of the subconscious to the truth of that which is declared to be true. Because of this quality of the subconscious there is nothing impossible to man. Whatever the mind of man can conceive and feel as true, the subconscious can and must objectify. Your feelings create the pattern from which your world is fashioned, and a change of feeling is a change of pattern.

The subconscious never fails to express that which has been impressed upon it. The moment it receives an impression, it begins to work out the ways of its expression. It accepts the feeling impressed upon it, your feeling, as a fact existing within itself and immediately sets about to produce in the outer or objective world the exact likeness of that feeling. The subconscious never alters the accepted beliefs of man. It out-pictures them to the last detail whether or not they are beneficial.

To impress the subconscious with the desirable state, you must assume the feeling that would be yours had you already realized your wish. In defining your objective, you must be concerned only with the objective itself. The manner of expression or the difficulties involved are not to be considered by you. To think feelingly on any state impresses it on the subconscious. Therefore, if you dwell on difficulties, barriers or delay, the subconscious, by its very non-selective nature, accepts the feeling of difficulties and obstacles as your request and proceeds to produce them in your outer world.

The subconscious is the womb of creation. It receives the idea unto itself through the feelings of man. It never changes the idea received, but always gives it form. Hence the subconscious out-pictures the idea in the image and likeness of the feeling received. To feel a state as hopeless or impossible is to impress the subconscious with the idea of failure.

Although the subconscious faithfully serves man, it must not be inferred that the relation is that of a servant to a master as was anciently conceived. The ancient prophets called it the slave and servant of man. St. Paul personified it as a "woman" and said: "The woman should be subject to man in everything" *(Ephesians 5:24; also, 1Corinthians 14:34, Ephesians 5:22, Colossians 3:18, 1Peter 3:1).* The subconscious does serve man and faithfully gives form to his feelings. However, the subconscious has a distinct distaste for compulsion and responds to persuasion rather than to command; consequently, it resembles the beloved wife more than the servant.

"The husband is head of the wife," Ephesians 5(:23), may not be true of man and woman in their earthly relationship, but it is true of the conscious and the subconscious, or the male and female aspects of consciousness. The mystery to which Paul referred when he wrote, "This is a great mystery *(5:32)* . . . He that loveth his wife loveth himself *(5:28)* . . . And they two shall be one flesh *(5:31)*", is simply the mystery of consciousness. Consciousness is really one and undivided but for creation's sake it appears to be divided into two.

The conscious (objective) or male aspect truly is the head and dominates the subconscious (subjective) or female aspect. However, this leadership is not that of the tyrant, but of the lover. So, by assuming the feeling that would be yours were you already in possession of your objective, the subconscious is moved to build the exact likeness of your assumption. Your desires are not subconsciously accepted until you assume the feeling of their reality, for only through feeling is an idea subconsciously accepted and only through this subconscious acceptance is it ever expressed.

It is easier to ascribe your feeling to events in the world than to admit that the conditions of the world reflect your feeling. However, it is eternally true that the outside mirrors the inside. "As within, so without" (*"As above, so below; as below, so above; as within, so without; as without, so within"*, *"Correspondence"*, *the second of The Seven Principles of Hermes Trismegistus*). "A man can receive nothing unless it is given him from heaven" *(John 3:27)* and "The kingdom of heaven is within you" *(Luke 17:21)*. Nothing comes from without; all things come from within – from the subconscious. It is impossible for you to see other than the contents of your consciousness. Your world in its every detail is your consciousness objectified. Objective states bear witness of subconscious impressions. A change of impression results in a change of expression.

The subconscious accepts as true that which you feel as true, and because creation is the result of subconscious impressions, you, by your feeling, determine creation. You are already that which you want to be, and your refusal to believe this is the only reason you do not see it.

To seek on the outside for that which you do not feel you are is to seek in vain, for we never find that which we want; we find only that which we are. In short, you express and have only that which you are conscious of being or possessing. "To him that hath it is given" *(Matthew 13:12; 25:29; Mark 4:25; Luke 8:18; 19:26).* Denying the evidence of the senses and appropriating the feeling of the wish fulfilled is the way to the realization of your desire.

Mastery of self-control of your thoughts and feelings is your highest achievement. However, until perfect self-control is attained, so that, in spite of appearances, you feel all that you want to feel, use sleep and prayer to aid you in realizing your desired states. These are the two gateways into the subconscious.

Chapter 2

Sleep

Sleep, the life that occupies one-third of our stay on earth, is the natural door into the subconscious. So it is with sleep that we are now concerned. The conscious two-thirds of our life on earth is measured by the degree of attention we give sleep. Our understanding of and delight in what sleep has to bestow will cause us, night after night, to set out for it as though we were keeping an appointment with a lover.

"In a dream, in a vision of the night, when deep sleep falleth upon men, in slumbering upon the bed; then he openeth the ears of men and sealeth their instruction", Job 33. It is in sleep and in prayer, a state akin to sleep, that man enters the subconscious to make his impressions and receive his instructions. In these states the conscious and subconscious are creatively joined. The male and female become one flesh. Sleep is the time when the male or conscious mind turns from the world of sense to seek its lover or subconscious self. The subconscious – unlike the woman of the world who marries her husband to change him – has no desire to change the conscious, waking state, but loves it as it is and faithfully reproduces its likeness in the outer world of form. The conditions and events of your life are your children formed from the molds of your subconscious impressions in sleep. They are made in the image and likeness of your innermost feeling that they may reveal you to yourself.

"As in heaven, so on earth" *(Matthew 6:10; Luke 11:2)*. As in the subconscious, so on earth. Whatever you have in consciousness as you go to sleep is the measure of your expression in the waking two-thirds of your life on earth. Nothing stops you from realizing your objective save your failure to feel that you are already that which you wish to be, or that you are already in possession of the thing sought. Your subconscious gives form to your desires only when you feel your wish fulfilled.

The unconsciousness of sleep is the normal state of the subconscious. Because all things come from within yourself, and your conception of yourself determines that which comes, you should always feel the wish fulfilled before you drop off to sleep. You never draw out of the deep of yourself that which you want; you always draw that which you are, and you are that which you feel yourself to be as well as that which you feel as true of others.

To be realized, then, the wish must be resolved into the feeling of being or having or witnessing the state sought. This is accomplished by assuming the feeling of the wish fulfilled. The feeling which comes in response to the question "How would I feel were my wish realized?" is the feeling which should monopolize and immobilize your attention as you relax into sleep. You must be in the consciousness of being or having that which you want to be or to have before you drop off to sleep.

Once asleep, man has no freedom of choice. His entire slumber is dominated by his last waking concept of self. It follows, therefore, that he should always assume the feeling of accomplishment and satisfaction before he retires in sleep, "Come before me with singing and thanksgiving" *(Psalm 95:2)*, "Enter into his gates with thanksgiving and into his courts with praise" *(Psalm 100:4)*. Your mood prior to sleep defines your state of consciousness as you enter into the presence of your everlasting lover, the subconscious. She sees you exactly as you feel yourself to be. If, as you prepare for sleep, you assume and maintain the consciousness of success by feeling "I am successful", you must be successful. Lie flat on your back with your head on a level with your body. Feel as you would were you in possession of your wish and quietly relax into unconsciousness.

"He that keepeth Israel shall neither slumber nor sleep" *(Psalm 121:4)*. Nevertheless "He giveth his beloved sleep" *(Psalm 127:2)*. The subconscious never sleeps. Sleep is the door through which the conscious, waking mind passes to be creatively joined to the subconscious.

Sleep conceals the creative act, while the objective world reveals it. In sleep, man impresses the subconscious with his conception of himself.

What more beautiful description of this romance of the conscious and subconscious is there than that told in the "Song of Solomon": "By night on my bed I sought him whom my soul loveth *(3:1)* . . . I found him whom my soul loveth; I held him and I not let him go, until I had brought him into my mother's house, and into the chamber of her that conceived me" *(3:4)*.

Preparing to sleep, you feel yourself into the state of the answered wish, and then relax into unconsciousness. Your realized wish is he whom you seek. By night, on your bed, you seek the feeling of the wish fulfilled that you may take it with you into the chamber of her that conceived you, into sleep or the subconscious which gave you form, that this wish also may be given expression. This is the way to discover and conduct your wishes into the subconscious. Feel yourself in the state of the realized wish and quietly drop off to sleep.

Night after night, you should assume the feeling of being, having and witnessing that which you seek to be, possess and see manifested. Never go to sleep feeling discouraged or dissatisfied. Never sleep in the consciousness of failure. Your subconscious, whose natural state is sleep, sees you as you believe yourself to be, and whether it be good, bad or indifferent, the subconscious will faithfully embody your belief. As you feel so do you impress her; and she, the perfect lover, gives form to these impressions and out-pictures them as the children of her beloved.

"Thou art all fair, my love; there is no spot in thee" *(Song of Solomon 4:7)* is the attitude of mind to adopt before dropping off to sleep. Disregard appearances and feel that things are as you wish them to be, for "He calleth things that are not seen as though they were, and the unseen becomes seen" *(Approx., Romans 4:17)*. To assume the feeling of satisfaction is to call conditions into being which will mirror satisfaction.

"Signs follow, they do not precede".

Proof that you are will follow the consciousness that you are; it will not precede it. You are an eternal dreamer dreaming non-eternal dreams. Your dreams take form as you assume the feeling of their reality. Do not limit yourself to the past. Knowing that nothing is impossible to consciousness, begin to imagine states beyond the experiences of the past.

Whatever the mind of man can imagine, man can realize. All objective (visible) states were first subjective (invisible) states, and you called them into visible by assuming the feeling of their reality. The creative process is first imagining and then believing the state imagined. Always imagine and expect the best.

The world cannot change until you change your conception of it. "As within, so without". Nations, as well as people, are only what you believe them to be. No matter what the problem is, no matter where it is, no matter whom it concerns, you have no one to change but yourself, and you have neither opponent nor helper in bringing about the change within yourself. You have nothing to do but convince yourself of the truth of that which you desire to see manifested. As soon as you succeed in convincing yourself of the reality of the state sought, results follow to confirm your fixed belief. You never suggest to another the state which you desire to see him express; instead, you convince yourself that he is already that which you desire him to be.

Realization of your wish is accomplished by assuming the feeling of the wish fulfilled. You cannot fail unless you fail to convince yourself of the reality of your wish. A change of belief is confirmed by a change of expression. Every night, as you drop off to sleep, feel satisfied and spotless, for your subjective lover always forms the objective world in the image and likeness of your conception of it, the conception defined by your feeling.

The waking two-thirds of your life on earth ever corroborates or bears witness to your subconscious impressions. The actions and events of the day are effects; they are not causes. Free will is only freedom of choice.

"Choose ye this day whom ye shall serve" *(Joshua 24:15)* is your freedom to choose the kind of mood you assume; but the expression of the mood is the secret of the subconscious. The subconscious receives impressions only through the feelings of man and, in a way known only to itself, gives these impressions form and expression. The actions of man are determined by his subconscious impressions. His illusion of free will, his belief in freedom of action, is but ignorance of the causes which make him act. He thinks himself free because he has forgotten the link between himself and the event.

Man awake is under compulsion to express his subconscious impressions. If in the past he unwisely impressed himself, then let him begin to change his thought and feeling, for only as he does so will he change his world. Do not waste one moment in regret, for to think feelingly of the mistakes of the past is to reinfect yourself. "Let the dead bury the dead" *(Matthew 8:22; Luke 9:60)*. Turn from appearances and assume the feeling that would be yours were you already the one you wish to be.

Feeling a state produces that state. The part you play on the world's stage is determined by your conception of yourself. By feeling your wish fulfilled and quietly relaxing into sleep, you cast yourself in a star role to be played on earth tomorrow, and, while asleep, you are rehearsed and instructed in your part.

The acceptance of the end automatically wills the means of realization. Make no mistake about this. If, as you prepare for sleep, you do not consciously feel yourself into the state of the answered wish, then you will take with you into the chamber of her who conceived you the sum total of the reactions and feelings of the waking day; and while asleep, you will be instructed in the manner in which they will be expressed tomorrow. You will rise believing that you are a free agent, not realizing that every action and event of the day is predetermined by your concept of self as you fell asleep. Your only freedom, then, is your freedom of reaction. You are free to choose how you feel and react to the day's drama, but the drama –

the actions, events and circumstances of the day – have already been determined.

Unless you consciously and purposely define the attitude of mind with which you go to sleep, you unconsciously go to sleep in the composite attitude of mind made up of all feelings and reactions of the day. Every reaction makes a subconscious impression and, unless counteracted by an opposite and more dominant feeling, is the cause of future action.

Ideas enveloped in feeling are creative actions. Use your divine right wisely. Through your ability to think and feel, you have dominion over all creation.

While you are awake, you are a gardener selecting seed for your garden, but "Except a corn of wheat fall into the ground and die, it abideth alone; but if it die, it bringeth forth much fruit" *(John 12:24)*. Your conception of yourself as you fall asleep is the seed you drop into the ground of the subconscious. Dropping off to sleep feeling satisfied and happy compels conditions and events to appear in your world which confirm these attitudes of mind.

Sleep is the door into heaven. What you take in as a feeling you bring out as a condition, action, or object in space. So sleep in the feeling of the wish fulfilled.

"As in consciousness, so on earth."

Chapter 3

Prayer

Prayer, like sleep, is also an entrance into the subconscious. "When you pray, enter into your closet, and when you have shut your door, pray to your Father which is in secret and your Father which is in secret shall reward you openly" *(Matthew 6:6)*.

Prayer is an illusion of sleep which diminishes the impression of the outer world and renders the mind more receptive to suggestion from within. The mind in prayer is in a state of relaxation and receptivity akin to the feeling attained just before dropping off to sleep.

Prayer is not so much what you ask for, as how you prepare for its reception. "Whatsoever things ye desire, when ye pray believe that you have received them, and ye shall have them" *(Mark 11:24)*.

The only condition required is that you believe that your prayers are already realized.

Your prayer must be answered if you assume the feeling that would be yours were you already in possession of your objective. The moment you accept the wish as an accomplished fact, the subconscious finds means for its realization. To pray successfully then, you must yield to the wish, that is, feel the wish fulfilled.

The perfectly disciplined man is always in tune with the wish as an accomplished fact.

He knows that consciousness is the one and only reality, that ideas and feelings are facts of consciousness and are as real as objects in space; therefore he never entertains a feeling which does not contribute to his happiness, for feelings are the causes of the actions and circumstances of his life.

On the other hand, the undisciplined man finds it difficult to believe that which is denied by the senses and usually accepts or rejects solely on appearances of the senses. Because of this tendency to rely on the evidence of the senses, it is necessary to shut them out before starting to pray, before attempting to feel that which they deny. Whenever you are in the state of mind "I should like to, but I cannot", the harder you try, the less you are able to yield to the wish. You never attract that which you want, but always attract that which you are conscious of being.

Prayer is the art of assuming the feeling of being and having that which you want. When the senses confirm the absence of your wish, all conscious effort to counteract this suggestion is futile and tends to intensify the suggestion.

Prayer is the art of yielding to the wish and not the forcing of the wish. Whenever your feeling is in conflict with your wish, feeling will be the victor. The dominant feeling invariably expresses itself. Prayer must be without effort. In attempting to fix an attitude of mind which is denied by the senses, effort is fatal.

To yield successfully to the wish as an accomplished fact, you must create a passive state, a kind of reverie or meditative reflection similar to the feeling which precedes sleep. In such a relaxed state, the mind is turned from the objective world and easily senses the reality of a subjective state. It is a state in which you are conscious and quite able to move or open your eyes but have no desire to do so. An easy way to create this passive state is to relax in a comfortable chair or on a bed. If on a bed, lie flat on your back with your head on a level with your body, close the eyes and imagine that you are sleepy. Feel – I am sleepy, so sleepy, so very sleepy.

In a little while, a faraway feeling accompanied by a general lassitude and loss of all desire to move envelops you. You feel a pleasant, comfortable rest and not inclined to alter your position, although under other circumstances you would not be at all comfortable. When this passive state is reached, imagine that you have realized your wish – not how it was realized, but simply the wish fulfilled. Imagine in picture form what you desire to achieve in life; then feel yourself as having already achieved it. Thoughts produce tiny little speech movements which may be heard in the passive state of prayer as pronouncements from without. However, this degree of passivity is not essential to the realization of your prayers. All that is necessary is to create a passive state and feel the wish fulfilled.

All you can possibly need or desire is already yours. You need no helper to give it to you; it is yours now. Call your desires into being by imagining and feeling your wish fulfilled. As the end is accepted, you become totally indifferent as to possible failure, for acceptance of the end wills the means to that end. When you emerge from the moment of prayer, it is as though you were shown the happy and successful end of a play although you were not shown how that end was achieved. However, having witnessed the end, regardless of any anticlimactic sequence, you remain calm and secure in the knowledge that the end has been perfectly defined.

Chapter 4

Spirit — Feeling

"Not by might, nor by power, but by my spirit, saith the Lord of hosts"
(Zechariah 4:6).

Get into the spirit of the state desired by assuming the feeling that would be yours were you already the one you want to be. As you capture the feeling of the state sought, you are relieved of all effort to make it so, for it is already so. There is a definite feeling associated with every idea in the mind of man. Capture the feeling associated with your realized wish by assuming the feeling that would be yours were you already in possession of the thing you desire, and your wish will objectify itself.

Faith is feeling, "According to your faith (feeling) be it unto you" *(Matthew 9:29).* You never attract that which you want, but always that which you are. As a man is, so does he see. "To him that hath it shall be given and to him that hath not it shall be taken away..." *(Matthew 13:12; 25:29; Mark 4:25; Luke 8:18; 19:26).* That which you feel yourself to be you are, and you are given that which you are. So assume the feeling that would be yours were you already in possession of your wish, and your wish must be realized. "So God created man in his own image, in the image of God created he him" *(Genesis 1:27).* "Let this mind be in you which was also in Christ Jesus, who being in the form of God, thought it not robbery to be equal with God" *(Philippians 2:5,6).* You are that which you believe yourself to be.

Instead of believing in God or in Jesus – believe you are God or you are Jesus. "He that believeth on Me, the works that I do shall he do also" *(John 14:12)* should be "He that believes as I believe the works that I do shall he do also". Jesus found it not strange to do the works of God, because He believed Himself to be God. "I and My Father are one" *(John 10:30)*. It is natural to do the works of the one you believe yourself to be. So live in the feeling of being the one you want to be and that you shall be.

When a man believes in the value of the advice given him and applies it, he establishes within himself the reality of success.

The Strangest Secret *in the* World

Earl Nightingale

Table *of* Contents

Text *of* Audio Version   25

Text *of* Video Version   45

Text *of* Audio Version

I'd like to tell you about The Strangest Secret in the World.

The late Nobel prize-winning Dr. Albert Schweitzer was once asked, "Doctor, what is wrong with men today?" The great doctor was silent a moment, and then he said, "Men simply do not think!" It is about this that I want to talk with you.

We live today in a golden age. This is an era that humanity has looked forward to, dreamed of, and worked toward for thousands of years. But since it is here we pretty well take it for granted. We are fortunate to live in the richest era that ever existed on the face of the earth. A land of abundant opportunity for everyone. But do you know what happens?

Let's take 100 individuals who start even at the age of 25.

Do you have any idea what will happen to those men and women by the time they are 65?

These 100 people, who all start even at the age of 25, all believe they're going to be successful. If you ask any one of them if they want to be a success they would tell you they did. You would notice that they are eager toward life, there is a certain sparkle in their eye, an erectness to their carriage. Life seems like a pretty interesting adventure to them.

But by the time they are 65, only one will be rich, four will be financially independent, 41 will still be working, and 54 will be broke - depending on others for life's necessities.

Now think a moment: Out of the 100, only five make the grade!

- Why do so many fail?
- What has happened to the sparkle that was there when they were 25?
- What has become of their dreams, their hopes, their plans?
- Why is there such a large disparity between what these people intended to do and what they actually accomplished?

The Definition of Success

When we say about 5% achieve success, we have to define success. Here is the best definition I've ever been able to find: *"Success is the progressive realization of a worthy ideal."*

If someone is working toward a predetermined goal and knows where they are going, that person is a success. If they are not doing that, they are a failure.

"Success is the progressive realization of a worthy ideal."

Rollo May, the distinguished psychiatrist, wrote in his wonderful book called: "Man's Search for Himself". *"The opposite of courage in our society is not cowardice - it is conformity."*

And there you have the trouble today; the reason for so many failures. Conformity ... people acting like everyone else, without knowing why or without knowing where they are going.

Now think of it.
Right now in America, there are over 40 million people 65 years of age and older.
And most of them are broke.
They are dependent on someone else for life's necessities.

- We learn to read by the time we are seven.
- We learn to make a living by the time we're 25.
- Often by that time we are not only making a living, we're supporting a family.
- And yet by the time we are 65, we have not learned how to become financially independent in the richest land that has ever been known.

Why?
We conform.
The trouble is most of us are acting like the wrong percentage group - the 95 who do not succeed.

Why do people conform?
Well, they really don't know. Most people seem to believe their lives are shaped by circumstances, by things that happen to them by exterior forces. They are outer directed people.

A survey was made one time that covered a lot of people, working people. These people were asked, "Why do you work?" "Why do you get up in the morning?"

19 out of 20 had no idea.

If you press them they will say, "Everyone goes to work in the morning." And that is the reason they do it - because everyone else is doing it.

Now let's get back to our definition of success. Who succeeds? The only person who succeeds is the person who is progressively realizing a worthy ideal. It is the person who says, "I am going to become this", and then begins to work towards that goal.

I'll tell you the successful people are.

- A success is the schoolteacher who is teaching school because that's what he or she wants to do.
- A success is the woman who is a wife and mother because she wanted to become a wife and mother and is doing a good job of it.
- A success is the man who runs the corner gas station because that was his dream.
- A success is the entrepreneur who starts their own company because that was their dream - that's what they wanted to do.
- A success is the successful salesperson who wants to become a top-notch salesperson and grow and build within his or her organization and sets forth on the pursuit of that goal.

A success is anyone who is pursuing deliberately a predetermined goal, because that's what he or she decided to do ... deliberately. But only one out of 20 does that. The rest are "failures."

That is why today there is really not any competition unless we make it for ourselves. Instead of competing, all we have to do is create.

For twenty years I looked for the key which would determine what would happen to a human being. I wanted to know if there was a key that would make the future a promise that we could foretell to a large extent.

Was there a key that would guarantee a person's becoming successful if they only knew about it and knew how to use it? *Well there is such a key and I have found it.*

Goals

Have you ever wondered why so many people work so hard and honestly without ever achieving anything in particular? And why others don't seem to work hard, yet seem to get everything? They seem to have the "magic touch." You've heard people say about someone, "Everything he touches turns to gold."

Have you ever noticed that a person who becomes successful tends to continue to become more successful? On the other hand, have you noticed how someone who is a failure tends to continue to fail?

The difference is goals. Some of us have goals, some don't. People with goals succeed because they know where they are going.

It's that simple.

Failures, on the other hand, believe that their lives are shaped by circumstances ... by things that happen to them ... by exterior forces.

Think of a ship leaving a harbor.
Think of it with the complete voyage mapped out and planned. The captain and crew know exactly where the ship is going and how long it will take - it has a definite goal. And 9,999 times out of 10,000, it will get to where it started out to get.

Now let's take another ship, just like the first, only let's not put a crew on it, or a captain at the helm. Let's give it no aiming point, no goal, and no destination. We just start the engines and let it go. I think you'll agree with me that if it gets out of the harbor at all, it will either sink or wind up on some deserted beach - a derelict. It can't go any place because it has no destination and no guidance.

It's the same with a human being.

Take the salesman for example.
There is no other person in the world today with the future of a good salesperson! Selling is the world's highest paid profession, if you are good

at it and if you know where you are going. Every company needs top notched salespeople. And they reward those people, the sky is the limit for them. But how many can you find?

Someone once said the human race is fixed. Not to prevent the strong from winning, but to prevent the weak from losing.

Western society today can be likened to a naval convoy in time of war. The entire economy is slowed down to protect its weakest link, just as the convoy has to go at the speed that will permit its slowest vessel to remain in formation.

That's why it's so easy to make a living today. It takes no particular brains or talent to make a living and support a family today. We have a plateau of so-called "security", if that is what a person is looking for. But we all do have to decide how high above this plateau we want to aim.

Now let's get back to the Strangest Secret in The World, the story I wanted to tell you today.

Why do those with goals succeed in life, and those without them fail? Well let me tell you something which, if you really understand it, will alter your life immediately. If you understand completely what I'm about to tell you from this moment on, your life will never be the same again.

You will suddenly find that good luck just seems to be attracted to you. The things you want just seem to fall in line. And from now on you won't have the problems, the worries, the gnawing lump of anxiety that perhaps you have experienced before. Doubt and fear will now be things of the past.

Here is the key to success, and, the key to failure.

"We become what we think about"

Let me say that again.

"We become what we think about"

Throughout history, the great wise men and teachers, philosophers, and prophets have disagreed with one another on many different things. It is only on this one point that they are in complete and unanimous agreement - the key to success and the key to failure is this:

The Strangest Secret

"We become what we think about"

Listen to what Marcus Aurelius, the great Roman Emperor, said: "A man's life is what his thoughts make of it."
Benjamin Disraeli said this: "Everything comes if a man will only wait ... I've brought myself, by long meditation, to the conviction that a human being with a settled purpose must accomplish it, and nothing can resist a will which will stake even existence upon its fulfillment."

Ralph Waldo Emerson said this, "A man is what he thinks about all day long."

William James said: "The greatest discovery of my generation is that human beings can alter their lives by altering their attitudes of mind."

And he said, "We need only in cold blood act as if the thing in question were real, and it will become infallibly real by growing into such a connection with our life that it will become real. It will become so knit with habit and emotion that our interests in it will be those which characterize belief."

He also said,
- "If you only care enough for a result, you will almost certainly obtain it."
- "If you wish to be rich, you will be rich."
- "If you wish to be learned, you will be learned."
- "If you wish to be good, you will be good."

He continues though,
" ... only you must, then, really wish these things, and wish them exclusively, and not wish at the same time a hundred other incompatible things just as strongly."

In the Bible you will read in Mark 9-23:
"If thou canst believe, all things are possible to him that believeth."

My old friend Dr. Norman Vincent Peale put it this way:
"This is one of the greatest laws in the universe. Fervently do I wish I had discovered it as a very young man. It dawned upon me much later in life, and I found it to be the greatest discovery, if not my greatest discovery outside my relationship to God."

The great law briefly and simply stated is:
- "If you think in negative terms, you will get negative results."
- "If you think in positive terms, you will achieve positive results."

"That simple fact," he went on to say, "is the basis of an astonishing law of prosperity and success." In three words:

"Believe and Succeed."

William Shakespeare put it this way,
"Our doubts are traitors and make us lose the good we oft might win by fearing to attempt."

George Bernard Shaw said:
"People are always blaming their circumstances for what they are. I don't believe in circumstances. The people who get on in this world are the people who get up and look for the circumstances they want, and if they can't find them, make them.

Well, it's pretty apparent, isn't it? And every person who discovered this, for a while, believed that they were the first to work it out.

"We become what we think about."

It stands to reason that a person who is thinking about a concrete and worthwhile goal is going to reach it, because that's what he's thinking about. And we become what we think about.

Conversely, the person who has no goal, who doesn't know where they are going, and whose thoughts must therefore be thoughts of confusion, anxiety, fear, and worry becomes what they think about. Their life becomes one of frustration, fear, anxiety, and worry.

And if we think about nothing ... we become nothing.

Now how does it work?
Why do we become what we think about?

Well I'll tell you how it works as far as we know. To do this I want to talk about a situation that parallels the human mind.

The Strangest Secret

As Ye Sow, So Shall Ye Reap

The human mind is much like a farmer's land.
Suppose a farmer has some land. And it is good, fertile land. The land gives the farmer a choice. He may plant in that land whatever he chooses. The land doesn't care what is planted. It's up to the farmer to make the decision.

Remember we are comparing the human mind to the farmers land because, the mind, like the land, doesn't care what you plant in it. It will return what you plant, but it doesn't care what you plant.

Let's say that the farmer has two seeds in his hand - one a seed of corn, the other is nightshade, a deadly poison. He digs two little holes in the earth and he plants both seeds, one corn, the other nightshade.

He covers up the holes, waters, and takes care of the land. What will happen? Invariably, the land will return what is planted. As it is written in the Bible, "*As ye sow, so shall ye reap.*"

Remember, the land doesn't care.
It will return poison in just as wonderful abundance as it will corn. So up come the two plants - one corn, one poison.
The human mind is far more fertile, far more incredible and mysterious than the land, but it works the same way. It does not care what we plant... success... or failure. A concrete, worth-while goal... or confusion, misunderstanding, fear, anxiety, and so on. But what we plant it must return to us.

The human mind is the last great unexplored continent on earth. It contains riches beyond our wildest dreams. It will return anything we want to plant.

So you may say, if that is true, why don't people use their minds more? Well I think they've figured out an answer to that one too.

The problem is that our mind comes as standard equipment at birth. It's free. And things that are given to us for nothing, we place little value on. Things that we pay money for, we value.

The paradox is that exactly the reverse is true.
Everything that's really worthwhile in life came to us free: our minds, our souls, our bodies, our hopes, our dreams, our ambitions, our intelligence, our love of family and children and friends and country.

All these priceless possessions are free.

But the things that cost us money are actually very cheap and can be replaced at any time. A good man can be completely wiped out and make another fortune. He can do that several times. Even if our home burns down, we can rebuild it. But the things we got for nothing, we can never replace.

The human mind is not used because we take it for granted. "Familiarity breeds contempt". It can do any kind of job we assign to it, but generally speaking, we use it for little jobs instead of big important ones. Universities have proved that most of us are operating on about ten percent or less of our abilities.

So decide now.
    What is it you want?
    Plant your goal in your mind.
    It's the most important decision you'll ever make in your entire life.
    What is it you want?

- Do you want to be an outstanding salesman?
- Do you want to excel at your particular job?
- Do you want to go places in your company? ... in your community?
- Do you want to be rich?

All you have got to do is plant that seed in your mind, care for it, work steadily towards your goal, and it will become a reality.

It not only will, there's no way that it cannot. You see, that's a law - like the laws of Sir Isaac Newton, the laws of gravity. If you get on top of a building and jump off, you'll always go down - you'll never go up. And it's the same with all the other laws of nature.

They are inflexible.
They always work.

Think about your goal in a relaxed, positive way.
Picture yourself in your mind's eye as having already achieved this goal. See yourself doing the things you will be doing when you have reached your goal.

The Strangest Secret

Ours has been called a Phenobarbital Age, the age of ulcers and nervous breakdowns and tranquilizers at a time when medical research has raised us to a new plateau of good health and longevity, far too many of us worry ourselves into an early grave trying to cope with things in our own little personal ways, without learning a few great laws that will take care of everything for us.

These things we bring on ourselves through our habitual way of thinking. Every one of us is the sum total of our own thoughts.

We are where we are because that is exactly where we really want or feel we deserve to be - whether we'll admit that or not.

Each of us must live off the fruit of our thoughts in the future, because what you think today and tomorrow - next month and next year - will mold your life and determine your future. You are guided by your mind.

I remember one time I was driving through eastern Arizona. I saw one of those giant earth-moving machines roaring along the road at about 35 miles an hour with what looked like 30 tons of dirt in it - a tremendous, incredible machine - and there was a little man perched way up on top with the wheel in his hands, guiding it. As I drove along I was struck by the similarity of that machine to the human mind.

Just suppose you are sitting at the controls of such a vast source of energy. Are you going to sit back and fold your arms and let it run itself into a ditch? Or are you going to keep both hands firmly on the wheel and control and direct this power to a specific, worthwhile purpose?
It's up to you.

You are in the driver's seat.

You see, the very law that gives us success is a double-edged sword. We must control our thinking. The same rule that can lead people to lives of success, wealth, happiness, and all the things they ever dreamed of for themselves and their family

That very same law can lead them into the gutter.
It's all in how it is used: for success ... or for failure.

This is The Strangest Secret in the world.

Why do I say it's strange, and why do I call it a secret? Actually, it is not a secret at all.

It was first promulgated by some of the earliest wise men, and it appears again and again throughout the Bible. But very few people have learned it or understand it. That's why it's strange, and why for some equally strange reason it virtually remains a secret.

I believe you could go out and walk down the main street of your town and ask one person after another what the secret of success is and you probably would not run into one person in a month that could tell you. This information is enormously valuable to us if we really understand it and apply it. It is valuable to us not only for our own lives, but the lives of those around us, our families, employees, associates, and friends.

Life should be an exciting adventure.
It should never be a bore.

A person should work fully, be alive. You should be glad to get out of bed in the morning. You should be doing a job that you like to do because you do it well.

One time I heard Grove Patterson, the great late editor in chief of the Toledo Daily Blade make a speech. And as he concluded his speech he said something I've never forgotten. He said, "My years in the newspaper business have convinced me of several things. Among them, that people are basically good, and that we came from someplace and we are going someplace. So we should make our time here an exciting adventure. The architect of the universe did not build a stairway leading nowhere. The greatest teacher of all, the carpenter from the Plains of Galilee of all gave us the secret time and time again: As ye believe, so shall it be done - unto you."

30 Day Action Ideas *for* Putting
The Strangest Secret *to* Work *for* You

I've explained the Strangest Secret in the World, and how it works. Now I'd like to explain how you can prove to yourself the enormous returns possible in your own life by putting the secret to a practical test.

I want you to make a test that will last 30 days. It is not going to be easy, but if you will give it a good try, it will completely change your life for the better.

Back in the 17th Century, Sir Isaac Newton, the English mathematician and natural philosopher gave us the natural laws of physics, which apply as much to human beings as they do to the movement of bodies in the universe. And one of these laws is: "For every action, there is an equal and opposite reaction".

Simply stated as it applies to you and me, it means we can achieve nothing without paying the price.

The results of your 30-day experiment will be in direct proportion to the effort you put forth. To be a doctor, you must pay the price of long years of difficult study. To be successful in selling, and remember each of us succeeds in life to the extent of our ability to sell,

- selling our families on our ideas,
- selling education in schools,
- selling our children on the advantages of living a good and honest life,
- selling our associates and employees on the importance of being exceptional people.

Too of course, the profession of selling itself.

But to be successful in selling our way of the good life, we must be willing to pay the price. What is that price? Well it is many things.

First, it is understanding emotionally as well as intellectually that we literally become what we think about, that we must control our thoughts if we are to control our lives. It is understanding fully that: "*As ye sow, so shall ye reap.*"

Second, it is cutting away all fetters from the mind and permitting it to soar as it was divinely designed to do. It is the realization that your limitations are self-imposed, and the opportunities for you today are enormous beyond belief. It is rising above narrow-minded pettiness and prejudice.

And third, it is using all your courage to force yourself to think positively on your own problem.

To set a definite and clearly defined goal for yourself and

To let your marvelous mind think about your goal from all possible angles,

To let your imagination speculate freely upon many different possible solutions.

To refuse to believe that there are any circumstances sufficiently strong to defeat you in the accomplishment of your purpose.

To act promptly and decisively when your course is clear and to keep constantly aware of the fact that you are at this moment standing in the middle of your own "Acres of Diamonds" as Russel Conwell points out in his book.

And fourth, save at least ten cents of every dollar you earn.

It is also remembering that no matter what your present job, it has enormous possibilities, if you are willing to pay the price.

Let's go over the important points in the price each of us must pay to achieve the wonderful life that can be ours.
It is of course worth any price.

>   **One**: Think - You will become what you think about.
>   **Two**: Imagine - Remember the word imagination and let your mind begin to soar.
>   **Three**: Courage - Concentrate on your goal every day.
>   **Four**: Save - ten percent of what you earn.
>   **Five**: Action - Ideas are worthless unless we act on them.

Next, I'll outline the 30 day test I want you to make, keeping in mind that you have nothing to lose by making this test, and everything you could possibly want to gain.
There are two things that may be said about everyone:

>   1) Each of us wants something, and
>   2) Each of us is afraid of something.

For the next 30 days, follow each of these steps every day until you have achieved your goal.

First, write on a card what it is you want more than anything else.
>   It may be more money. Perhaps you'd like to double your income or make a specific amount of money.

The Strangest Secret

It may be a beautiful home.
It may be success at your job.
It may be a particular position in life.
It could be a more harmonious family.
Each of us wants something.

Write down on your card specifically what it is you want.
Make sure it's a single goal and clearly defined. You need not show it to anyone, in fact often it is best not to. (*Cast not your pearls before swine, lest they trample them, and turn again and rend you.* - Matthew 7)

Carry the card with you so that you can look at it several times a day. Think about your goals in a cheerful, relaxed, positive way each morning when you get up, and immediately you have something to work for - something to get out of bed for, something to live for.

Look at the goals written on your card every chance you get during the day and just before going to bed at night. As you look at it, remember that you must become what you think about, and since you're thinking about your goal, you realize that soon it will be yours.

In fact, it is really yours the moment you write it down and begin to think about it. Look at the abundance all around you as you as you go about your daily business. You have as much right to this abundance as any living creature. It is yours for the asking.

Now we come to the difficult part. Difficult because it means the formation of what is probably a brand-new habit. New habits are not easily formed. Once formed however, they will follow you for the rest of your life.

Second, stop thinking about what it is you fear.
Each time a fearful or negative thought comes into your conscious mind, replace it with a mental picture of your positive and worthwhile goal. And there will come times when you'll feel like giving up. It's easier for a human being to think negatively than positively. That's why only five percent are successful!

You must begin now to place yourself in that group. For 30 days you must take control of your mind. It will think about only what you permit it to think about. Each day for this 30-day test, do more than you have to do.

In addition to maintaining a cheerful positive outlook, give of yourself more than you have ever done before. Do this knowing that your returns in life must be in direct proportion to what you give.

The moment you decide on a goal to work toward, you immediately are a successful person. You are then in that rare and successful category of people who know where they are going. Out of every 100 people, you belong to the top five.

Don't concern yourself too much with how you are going to achieve your goal. Leave that completely to a power greater than yourself. The answers will come to you of their own accord and at the right time. (As Jiminy Cricket sings: "Like a bolt out of the blue, Fate steps in and sees you through!")

All you have to know is where you are going.

Remember these words from the sermon on the mount, and remember them well. Keep them constantly before you this month of your test.

> "Ask, And It Shall Be Given You"
> "Seek, And Ye Shall Find"
> "Knock, And It Shall Be Opened Unto You"
> "For Every One That Asketh Receiveth"

It is as marvelous and as simple as that. In fact it is so simple, that in our seemingly complicated world, it is difficult for an adult to understand that all they need is a purpose ... and faith.

For 30 days, do your very best.
If you are a salesman, go at it as you have never done before, not in a hectic fashion, but with the calm cheerful assurance that time well spent will give you the abundance in return that you want.

If you are a homemaker, devote your 30 day test to completely giving of yourself without thinking of receiving anything in return, and you will be amazed at the difference it makes in your life.

No matter what your job, do it as you have never done before, and if you have kept your goal before you every day for 30 days, you will wonder and marvel at this new life you have found.

Dorothea Brande, the outstanding editor and writer, discovered it for herself and talks about it in her fine book "Wake up and Live". Her entire philosophy is reduced to the words: "Act as though it were impossible to fail." She made her own test, with sincerity and faith, and her entire life was changed to overwhelming success.

Now, you make your test for 30 full days.

Don't start your test until you have made up your mind to stick with it. You see by being persistent, you are demonstrating faith. Persistence is simply another word for faith. If you did not have faith, you would never persist.

If you should fail within your first 30 days, by that I mean finding yourself overwhelmed by negative thoughts - you have to start over again from that point and go 30 more days.

Gradually, your new habit will form, until you find yourself one of that wonderful minority to whom virtually nothing is impossible.

And don't forget the card.
It is vitally important as you begin this new way of living.

On one side of the card, write your goal, whatever it may be. On the other side, write the words we've quoted from the sermon on the mount.

> "Ask, And It Shall Be Given You"
> "Seek, And Ye Shall Find"
> "Knock, And It Shall Be Opened Unto You"
> "For Every One That Asketh Receiveth"

In your spare time during your test period read books that will help you. Read at least 15 minutes each day. Inspirational books like The Bible, Dorothea Brand's "Wake up and Live" if you can still find a copy, "The Magic of Believing" by Claude Bristol, "Think and Grow Rich" by Napoleon Hill, and other books that instruct and inspire.

Nothing great was ever accomplished without inspiration. See that during these crucial first 30 days your own inspiration is kept to a peak.

Above all ... don't worry!

Worry brings fear, and fear is crippling. The only thing that can cause you to worry during your test is trying to do it all yourself. Know that all you have to do is hold your goal before you; everything else will take care of itself.

Remember also to keep calm and cheerful, don't let petty things annoy you and get you off course.

Now since making this test is difficult, some will say, "Why should I bother?"

> Well look at the alternative.
> No one wants to be a failure.
> No one really wants to be a mediocre individual.
> No one wants a life constantly full of fear and worry and frustration.

Therefore remember that you will reap that which you sow. If you sow negative thoughts, your life will be filled with negative things. If you sow positive thoughts, your life will be cheerful, successful, and positive.

Gradually you will have a tendency to forget what you have just learned. Read this again each week. Keep reminding yourself of what you must do to form this new habit. Gather your whole family around at regular intervals and listen to what has been said here.

Most people will tell you that they want to make money, without understanding the law. The only people who make money work in a mint. The rest of us must earn money.

This is what causes those who keep looking for something for nothing, or a free ride, to fail in life. The only way to earn money is by providing people with services or products which are needed and useful. We exchange our time and our product or service for the other person's money.

Therefore the law is that our financial return will be in direct proportion to our service.

Success is not the result of making money. Earning money is the result of success - and success is in direct proportion to our service.

Most people have this law backwards.

They believe that you are successful if you earn a lot of money. The truth is that you can only earn money after you are successful.

It's like the man who stands in front of the stove and says to it: "Give me heat and then I'll add the wood." How many men and women do you know, or do you suppose there are today, who take the same attitude toward life?

There are millions.

We've got to put the fuel in before we can expect heat. Likewise, we've got to be of service first before we can expect money.

Don't concern yourself with the money. Be of service ... build ... work ...dream ... create! Do this and you'll find there is no limit to the prosperity and abundance that will come to you.

Prosperity is founded upon a law of mutual exchange. Any person who contributes to prosperity must prosper in turn themselves.

Sometimes the return will not come from those you serve, but it must come to you from someplace, because that is the law.

For every action, there is an equal and opposite reaction.

As you go daily through your 30-day test period, your success will always be measured by the quality and quantity of service you render, and money is a yardstick for measuring this service. No person can get rich themselves, unless they first enrich others. There are no exceptions to a law.

You can drive down any street and from your car estimate the service that is being rendered by the people living on that street.

Have you ever thought of this yardstick before? It's interesting. Some, like ministers, priests and other devoted people measure their returns in the realm of the spiritual, but again their returns are equal to their service.

Once this law is understood, any thinking person can tell their own fortune. If they want more, they must be of more service to those he receives his return. If they want less, they have only to reduce their service. This is the price you must pay for what you want.

If you believe you can enrich yourself by deluding others, you can end only by deluding yourself. It may take some time, but as surely as you breathe, you will get back what you put out.

Don't ever make the mistake of thinking you can avert this. It's impossible: The prisons and the streets where the lonely walk are filled with people who tried to make new laws just for themselves. We may avoid the laws of men for a while, but there are greater laws that cannot be broken.

An outstanding medical doctor recently pointed out six steps that will help you realize success.

    1. Set yourself a definite goal.

    2. Quit running yourself down.

    3. Stop thinking of all the reasons why you cannot be successful and instead think of all the reasons why you can.

    4. Trace your attitudes back through your childhood and discover where you first got the idea that you could not be successful if that is the way you've been thinking.

    5. Change the image you have of yourself by writing out a description of the person you would like to be.

    6. Act the part of the successful person you have decided to become.

The doctor that wrote those words is a noted west coast psychiatrist, Dr. David Harold Fink.

Do what the experts since the dawn of recorded history have told you you must do: pay the price by becoming the person you want to become. It's not nearly as difficult as living unsuccessfully.

Take this 30-day test, then repeat it ... then repeat it again.

Each time it will become more a part of you until you'll wonder how you could have ever have lived any other way. Live this new way and the floodgates of abundance will open and pour over you more riches than you may have dreamed existed.

Money?
Yes, lots of it.

But what's more important, you'll have peace ... you'll be in that wonderful minority who lead calm, cheerful, successful lives.

Start today.
You have nothing to lose - but you have your whole life to win.

This is Earl Nightingale.
Thank you.

Text *of* Video Version

Introduction

Back in 1956, I wrote and recorded something we called the Strangest Secret. Without advertising or fanfare of any kind it outsold all other non-musical, non-entertainment type recordings. It has been heard by millions and millions of people throughout the free world and in the process created a brand-new industry: learning through listening, on one of these solid-state cassette tape players. This player has revolutionized the learning process. Now people listen in their automobiles while they are driving to and from work and on sales calls, time that was formerly wasted, on their commuter train with the little earpiece, in the bathroom while shaving in the morning, or at the dinner table with the children gathered around the table and the whole family together, for a change. This has made a tremendous difference in the business of learning.

But, getting back to the Strangest Secret. What makes it a best seller? What is it about that recording that caused millions and millions of people to want to hear it over and over again and let their children hear it and play it for their employees and sales forces. Well I'm making a talk here today in which I will cover the highlights and philosophy of the Strangest Secret, and I'd like to invite you to join us. I hope you find it of some value.

I want to tell you the most interesting story in the world. Why a person becomes the person they become. Why a little boy or a little girl grows up to be the kind of person he or she becomes.

The estimates by the experts in this field are that most of us are using somewhere around 5% of our real potential, some experts say as little as 1%.

It means that we are only giving about 5% of ourselves to what we are doing, to our days, our work, our families, everyone we know, our entire environment.

But it also means that we are only experiencing 5% of the fun, 5% of the joy, 5% of the rewards we could be knowing, or less.

All the experts are agreed that in each of us, there are deep reservoirs of ability, even genius, that we habitually fail to use.

Why?

We know that most people desire by nature to succeed. But what is success?

What is this word that has become so famous in the world?
What does it mean?

Most people do not know what success is all about, and since they do not know what it is about, they really don't know where to look for it.

Success is really nothing more than the progressive realization of a worthy ideal.
This means that any person who knows what they are doing and where they are going is a success. Any person with a goal towards which they are working is a successful person.

This means that a boy in high school working towards a diploma, the girl in college towards a degree, is just as successful as any human being on earth, because they know what they are doing, why they are getting up in the morning, and where they are going.

But conversely, if a person doesn't know what they are working toward, what it is they want, doesn't have a goal towards which they are working, then they, at least by this definition, be called unsuccessful.

Why isn't then, with this simple definition, why isn't everyone successful? It should be easy. Yet surveys indicate that 19 out of 20, 95% at least are not. In fact a survey one time asked thousands of working men why they got up in the morning and went to work, and 19 out of 20 didn't know.

19 out of 20 working people didn't have the foggiest notion why they got up in the morning and went to work. Under closer questioning they said, "Well, everyone works."

Well, that would be a good reason to quit. In fact, a little rule of thumb you might want to remember: Whatever the great majority is doing under any given circumstance, if you do exactly the opposite, you will probably never make another mistake as long as you live. Just something to keep in the back of your mind.

The problem with most people is that they are playing the world's most unrewarding game, and the name of the game is: Follow the Follower.

There is a story about a small town in which there was a jewelry store, and like all jewelry stores, or most jewelry stores at least, there was a big clock in their front window.

Every morning for years, the jeweler had noticed a working man stop, adjust his pocket watch to the same time as the clock in the window.

He has been doing this for many years. One morning the jeweler was out in front sweeping his sidewalk, and asked the man, "Why do you adjust your watch to my big clock every morning? I've noticed you doing that for years."
The man said, "Well I'm the foreman down at the big plant. I want to make sure my watch is correct because I blow the quitting whistle every night at 5 o'clock.

The jeweler looked at him rather strangely for a moment, and then he said, "Well that's funny, I've been setting that big clock in the window by that quitting whistle all these years."

A very logical thing, but between them they could have been off six months! It is a case of people just going along with what they thought to be correct without checking their references.

So I want to suggest that from now on out, at least we do that. That we check our references, and ask ourselves, "Are the people I'm following going where I want to go?"

Let me tell you the story of what we might call the average young man in our society. From the time this boy is born, there is only one thing on this earth he can do, and that is to begin to think, act, and talk like the people by whom he is surrounded. This is all in the world he can do.

But right off the bat, the odds are 95 to 5 that he is thinking, acting, and talking like the wrong group. They are wonderful people, they love him, they would do anything in the world for him, they want him to succeed, but the odds are 95 to 5 that they have not got the answers he needs if he is to reach fulfillment as a human being, if he is to reach this success that he wants, if he is to reach into the deep reservoirs of ability and genius we know he possesses and draw it out.

Well, he starts in school. The most important thing to a boy in school is to be liked by the other little boys in school. And so at this tender age he begins to follow other little boys his same age, who don't know any more than he knows, do not have his best interests at heart, and who do not necessarily have any capacity for leadership.

He does this in the first grade, and the second, and the third, and the fourth, and the fifth, and the sixth, and the seventh, and the eighth, and year after year after year he forms himself into a composite average of other little boys his age, trying to be like them. Trying to do the only thing in the world it is impossible for a human being to do, which is to be like somebody else.

Now let's say he goes all the way through school, and then usually he goes in the military service. Again he is caught in the viselike grip of conformity.

Now let's say he is 25 years old, out of school, out of the service. What's he going to do? As a rule, he will go back to his hometown, unless he is married in which case he will go to his wife's hometown, but let's say he goes back to his own hometown.

He is single. He doesn't know quite what to do. He is standing on a corner one morning and a friend that he knew in school comes up and says, "Hi there Charlie! What are you doing?"

He says, "Nothing." His friend says, "Why don't you come down and work where I work. It's a pretty good place, the pay is regular, we've got all kinds of fringe benefits... and so on." And so he does.

The odds are about again 95 to 5 that his first job is taken as a result of random application.

On the job, without thinking about it, the most natural thing in the world for him to do is to look around, see how the other guys are doing their job, and begin doing his the same way, assuming that what is normal for them is normal for him. No reason for this, he doesn't think about it, he just does it.

Now he has stretching in front of him fifty years or more in the golden age that man has been dreaming of since the days of ancient Greece. What is he going to do with these fifty golden years? Well let's take a good close look at him.

We know that he works 40 hours a week, as a rule. This leaves him 72 hours a week when he is neither working nor sleeping. 72 free discretionary hours each week to do with as he pleases.

Now at this point of course he is married and has his little house and little car. And this is about what he does with his free 72 hours every week. He'll do what the other guys are doing with their free 72 hours every week, which is virtually nothing at all.

On a typical day, he'll quit right on the dot, get in his little car, go to his little house, go in his little kitchen, kiss his little wife, and say I'm tired. They have even figured out why he says that. The experts believe that he used to hear his father say that back when men used to get tired working during the day and he picked it up and he repeats this every night when he gets home.

He bolts down his little meal and then he heads to the living room where he turns on his escape box. Click!

It takes 15-20 seconds for the screen to light up, a period of time he finds interminable, but he gets through it somehow, kicks the dog or thumbs through a magazine or something.

Then the screen lights up and he does too a little bit. There in front of him he sees people in all kinds of funny old-time costumes all killing each other at a great rate. Now one expert has agreed that the average family can see more death and bloodshed and carnage on the television set in a week than Crassus saw when he crucified 6000 prisoners on the southern road to Rome, but you know how those experts are, they can certainly be off one or two.

But he sits there for five or six hours. Twenty-five percent of all free time now is spent in front of the tube according to the latest statistics.

Now there is nothing wrong with this particularly, except that he is watching other people who are earning excellent incomes in the pursuit of their careers while he does not make a nickel, and gets one of the only two things you can get by watching TV on that kind of a schedule... red eyes and a hollow head.

This is not meant to be an indictment of television I've got a couple of television sets at home too. I've got a couple of cars at home too, but I don't go home at night and drive around the block for six hours! If there is someplace I want to go, fine, my car will take me there. If there is a great program, like a golf match or something like that, I want to see it.

But he sits there for five or six hours until finally his wife, who is a little more practical than him, taps him on the shoulder and says, "Charlie, I think it is about time you went to bed. You've got to get up in the morning and go to work." He says OK and shuts it off, he knows how to do that, he just shuts it off and goes to bed.

The next morning he gets up and he does this all over again. He does this every day for 40 years. At the end of 40 years he gets retired, which always kind of catches him by surprise, no one has ever figured that out either, and then he dies at 85 or 90, the way medical science is moving us along, out of sheer boredom.

Well what is the problem?
Is there a tragedy here? Not really if that is the way Charlie, our mythical, hypothetical young man, wants to spend his life. If he wants to spend his life that way, that is his business. He lives in a free society. He can do anything with his life that he wants.

But there is a terrible tragedy here if he is living that way because of a total lack of a decision. If he is living that way simply because he is still doing what he was doing in the first and second grade, and that is going along with all the fellows up and down the block on the unspoken assumption that they know how to live. Then there is a real tragedy there, because they have never known how to live, not in all the recorded history of mankind.

He never finds out who he is. He never reaches into the deep depths of his abilities, his talents. He never learns that he can have just about everything he wants in the world, that he can call his own shots, tell his own fortune. And it's kind of a pity.

www.ingramcontent.com/pod-product-compliance
Lightning Source LLC
Chambersburg PA
CBHW020525030426
42337CB00011B/553

*It is a small book but not slight.
There is a treasure in it,
a clearly defined road to the
realization of your dreams.*

Page 4

Well what is new? What is needed, I think, is a checklist like an airplane pilot uses. I think that living successfully is at least as important as flying an airplane. Here are some of the things that, I think, should be on that checklist, that could help this young man live a more interesting, more meaningful, more exciting, more enjoyable life.

The first thing that he ought to have on his checklist, in my opinion, is the word: "Goal". A man without a goal is like a ship without a rudder. He doesn't know where he is going. He then belongs to that 95% that are just living day by day, week after week, month after month like a starfish or an amoeba. He needs to know where he is going.

Back in the early days of navigation, sailors used to see a strange sight in the Antarctic. They used to see a giant iceberg towering high out of the sea, and it would be moving against the wind. The wind would be blowing one way and the iceberg would be moving right into the teeth of the wind. This frightened the sailors whose ships were powered by the wind, until it was discovered that only a fraction of the great iceberg was visible and its huge ponderous roots were caught in the great currents of the ocean. It was being carried purposely along its way regardless of the winds and the tides on the surface. This is what a man needs.

He needs his roots deep in the great mainstream of his own choosing, and then he'll move along his way regardless of the winds on the surface of his life or short-term expediency. And then he will get to where he is going.

A second word on our checklist might be the word: "Attitude". It has been called the most important word in any language in the world, because it is our attitude toward our world and toward all the people in it that will determine the world's attitude and all the people's attitude toward us. It is a simple thing, most of us know it but we tend to forget it. People will react to us according to our attitude. Our attitude is the greatest gift we can be given.

You know, the little creatures of the world were given a wonderful gift by Mother Nature called protective coloring which lets them blend into their background so they cannot be seen. But man was not given this great gift, because man was given an incalculably greater one. Only man has the godlike power to make his surroundings change to fit him, because his environment will change as he changes. A man's environment is a merciless mirror of him as a human being. If he thinks his environment could stand a little improvement, all he has to do is improve and his environment will improve to reflect the change in him.

Third would be the word: "Think". To think, the highest function of which a human being is capable. It was put pretty well by the great Pulitzer Prize winning playwright Archibald McLeish[1] in his great play "The Secret of Freedom" in which he has one of his characters saying, "The only thing about a man that is a man… is his mind. Everything else you can find in a pig or a horse." It's true!

And so, if we are going to develop something, this is a good place to start. To think deliberately, and with a purpose. To spend a little time each day before a blank sheet of paper with our goal perhaps written at the top. To come up with some fresh new exciting ideas.

Our checklist should include what you might call the law of laws. That's what Emerson called it. The great old law of cause and effect. That our rewards in life will always be in exact proportion to our contribution to our service. We all know this really. We tell our children in Sunday School, "*As Ye sow So Shall Ye Reap*", but we forget that that is true. If a man is unhappy with his rewards, all in the world that his has to do is find ways of increasing his contribution, his service.

It reminds me of the story of the preacher who was driving down a country road when he came upon the most magnificent farm he had ever seen in his life. It was beautiful. He saw the farmer approaching the road on his tractor, so he hailed him. "My good man, God has certainly blessed you with a magnificent farm." The farmer thought for a moment and replied, "Yes, you are right, he certainly has. But you should have seen this place when he had it all to himself." The preacher had his sermon for the next Sunday. He realized that all the farmers up and down that road had been given the same land, yet one man had made something great out of it.

Well all of us have been given the same land. We are given a human life, and each of us can make something great out of it too if we want.

The next point might be simply the word: "Truth." Since everything we do has an equal and opposite reaction, unless what we are doing is based on truth, we are building on sand, and it can't stand.

---

[1] *American poet, writer, and the Librarian of Congress. He is associated with the Modernist school of poetry. He received three Pulitzer Prizes for his work.*

Next would be R&D, research and development. None of us would want to work for a company, or invest our money in a company that did not have a very viable research and development department, that is pumping a good percentage of its profits back into research and development because its future depends on it. And so does a man's future depend on it.

You might ask yourself how much of your take home pay and discretionary time have you spent during the past year on materials calculated to make you smarter this year than you were the year before. Calculated to make you a little better, a little bigger as a human being. To perhaps love a little more, hate a little less, do a little better job than you did a year ago. How much time and money are you pumping back into yourself and your future? It's worth thinking about.

And finally, the Strangest Secret. At the beginning I asked, "What makes a child grow up to be the human being he becomes?" Well this is the reason for that.

Of course he is the confluence of a genetic pool that goes back for thousands and thousands of years. And his environment has an influence on him of course. But what makes him the person he becomes is that **he becomes what he thinks about most of the time**. It is as simple as that. We become what we think about most of the time. And that is the Strangest Secret.

This is why thinking is so vital. This is why a goal is so important. Because we will become that. This is why people who set goals achieve them. The trouble with men is not in achieving their goals, they do that. It is in establishing them.

Well that is about it. I think it is good to remember, if we just go along with the crowd, we won't wind up with much more than the wish that we could do it all over again, and as far as we know you can't. If we want to amount to anything as individuals, we need: individual goals, individual thinking, individual actions, and we must never conform to the big group. We must love them, We must help them, We must serve them because our entire success will depend on our ability to do these things, but never lose our individuality and our identity by permitting ourselves to become submerged in what has historically proved itself to be little more than a suffocating sea of indirection and purposelessness. If we want to emulate someone, fine, but let's be choosy in whose steps we follow. It's the only life we've got. And remember to think. Imagination is everything, and we can become what we can imagine.

If you find yourself getting depressed and down at the mouth, as we all get once in a while, you might want to remember this quotation by Dean Briggs. He said, "Do your work. Not just your work and no more, but a little more for the lavishing sake, that little more which is worth all the rest. And if you suffer as you must and you doubt as you must, do your work. Put your heart into it and the sky will clear. And then out of your very doubt and suffering will be born the supreme joy of life. Believe it or not, in an age where we've come to nearly deify leisure time, we have virtually lost sight of the fact that nearly all our satisfactions and rewards will come, not from our leisure, but from our work.

And don't forget "The Strangest Secret". We become what we think about.